Uncover the secrets behind amazing dinosaur facts!

DINOPEDIA

QEB

QEB Publishing

RUPERT MATTHEWS

CONTENTS

COMBAT

DINO GUIDE

Words in bold can be found in the glossary on page 113.

DINOSAUR DIG

Dinosaurs were **reptiles** that lived on the earth long before humans. They became **extinct** about 65 million years ago. There are no dinosaurs alive today.

Scientists called **paleontologists** (pay-lee-on-toll-oh-jists) study dinosaurs. By examining dinosaur remains, called **fossils**, paleontologists can show what dinosaurs looked like when they were alive.

▲ Paleontologist Jack Horner has excavated, or dug up, a nest of fossilized dinosaur eggs in the United States.

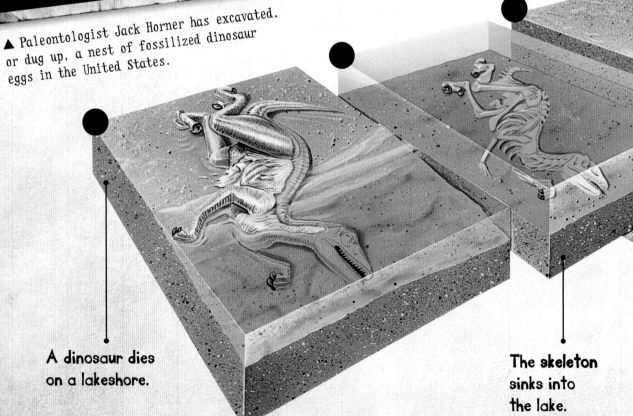

A dinosaur dies on a lakeshore.

The skeleton sinks into the lake.

Many dinosaur remains have been found—of all different types from several different times. These remains help paleontologists to understand how these creatures lived and behaved.

▼ When a plant or animal dies, it usually rots away completely. However, in special conditions, parts of it can become fossilized.

HOW BIG WERE DINOSAURS?

Every dinosaur is compared to an average adult to show just how big they really were.

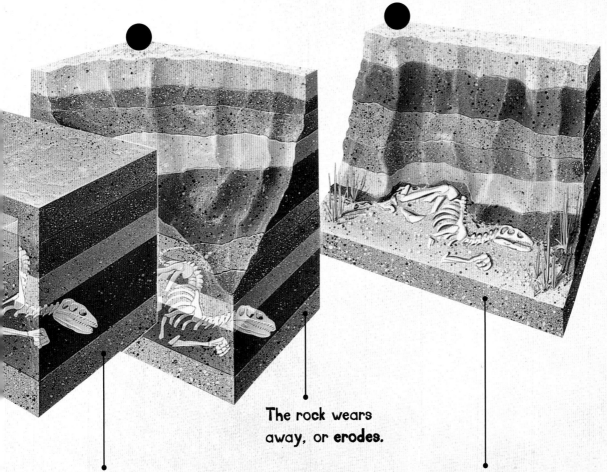

The rock wears away, or **erodes**.

Layers of mud settle over the skeleton. The mud and bones gradually turn into stone.

As more rock erodes, the skeleton is revealed.

FAMILIES

Did you know that eggs were hatched in nurseries?

Or that some dinosaurs lived in **herds** and some alone?

Read on to discover everything you need to know about dinosaur families...

CARING FOR THE EGGS

Dinosaurs laid eggs, which were kept warm and safe until they **hatched** into babies.

In hot areas, the eggs were laid on the warm ground. The mother dinosaur would stay nearby to provide shade from the sun if the eggs became too hot.

In cooler parts of the world, the mother dinosaur may have piled leaves on top of the eggs. As the leaves rotted, they produced heat, which kept the eggs warm.

DINOSAUR DIG

WHAT	Jobaria
WHERE	Niger, Africa
PERIOD	110 million years ago in the early **Cretaceous**

DIG SITE

WOW! In July 1923, Roy Chapman Andrews and his team found the first dinosaur eggs in Mongolia, Asia— they were Oviraptor (oh-vee-rap-tor) eggs.

65 ft (20 m)

JOBARIA

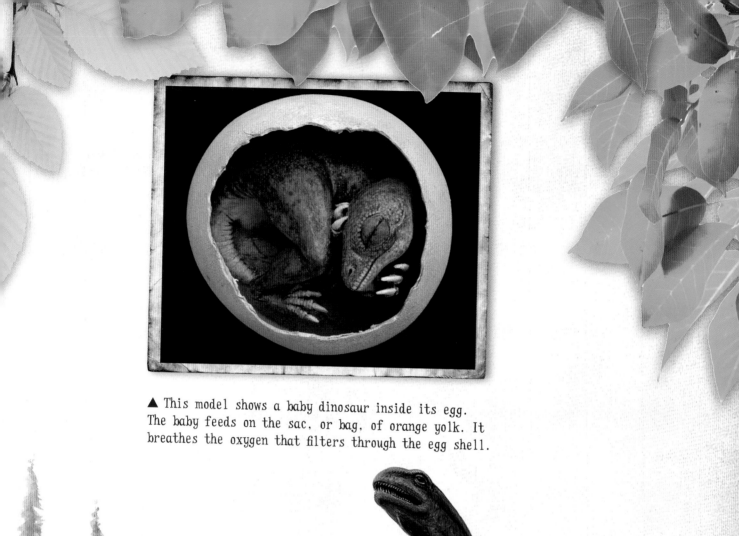

▲ This model shows a baby dinosaur inside its egg. The baby feeds on the sac, or bag, of orange yolk. It breathes the oxygen that filters through the egg shell.

◀ A mother Jobaria (joe-barr-ee-ah) tries to drive off a smaller hunting dinosaur. Many dinosaur eggs were eaten before they had a chance to hatch.

THE NURSERY

Some dinosaurs built large **nurseries** where more than 100 dinosaurs laid their eggs in nests close to each other.

After the eggs hatched, the **adult** dinosaurs brought food to their young and guarded the nursery from attack. The babies stayed in the nest for several weeks.

Hunting dinosaurs may have cared for their babies in a similar way. Young hunters probably followed their parents for several months so that they could learn how to hunt successfully.

DINOSAUR DIG

WHAT Maiasaura

WHERE Montana, North America

PERIOD 75 million years ago in the late Cretaceous

DIG SITE

▲ Maiasaura (my-yah-saw-rah) would hatch from their eggs after eight to ten weeks.

30 ft (9 m)

MAIASAURA

▶ The young Maiasaura stayed in the nursery for several weeks after they hatched, so they could be cared for by their parents.

11

YOUNGSTERS

Young animals, including dinosaurs,
look and behave differently from adults.

Their head and eyes are large in proportion to
their body—this makes their body look too
small! Their legs tend to be shorter and thicker
than those of adults.

Mussaurus (moo-saw-rus) had a
large head, large eyes, and short
legs. Scientists think that the
fossil they have found is of
a baby animal. The adult
would have been much larger
and looked different.

DINOSAUR DIG

WHAT	Mussaurus
WHERE	Argentina, South America
PERIOD	215 million years ago in the late Triassic

DIG SITE

▶ A baby Mussaurus would
only have been 8 inches
(20 centimeters) in length–
about the size of a rat.

WOW!

Fossils of a young
Tyrannosaurus (tie-rann-
oh-saw-rus) have been
found. The remains show
that it was probably a fierce
killer, just like the adult.

▲ The fossil of Mussaurus is one of the smallest dinosaur skeletons ever found, but it is of a baby. The adult would have been about 13 feet (4 meters) in length.

13 ft (4 m)

MUSSAURUS

LEAVING THE NEST

Not all dinosaurs cared for their young in nurseries. Some youngsters had to look after themselves.

Young sauropods, such as Apatosaurus (ap-at-oh-saw-rus), hid from hunters in bushes and other **undergrowth**. As they grew larger, the youngsters may have left the safety of cover as they were able to fight off attackers.

Fossil footprints show that sauropods waded into lakes or rivers. They may have been hiding or escaping from hunters.

DINOSAUR DIG

WHAT	Apatosaurus
WHERE	Wyoming, North America
PERIOD	150 million years ago in the late **Jurassic**

DIG SITE

▼ Young sauropods, such as Apatosaurus, left the nest when they were only a few days old. Adults collected soft plants for the babies to eat when they hatched, but then they ignored their young.

80 ft (25 m)

APATOSAURUS

WOW!

Fossils of Apatosaurus came from rocks of the Morrison Formation in the western U.S., which contains more dinosaur fossils than any other rocks on earth.

LIFE SKILLS

Some scientists believe that baby dinosaurs sometimes followed their parents instead of living by themselves.

A young dinosaur relied on its parents for protection against attack. The youngster would have learned many skills by watching its parents, including which plants were good to eat, which food to avoid, and which dinosaurs were dangerous hunters.

DINOSAUR DIG

WHAT Cetiosaurus
WHERE England, Europe
PERIOD 180 million years ago in the mid-Jurassic

DIG SITE

▶ The backbone of Cetiosaurus (set-ee-oh-saw-rus) looks similar to a whale's, which is why the creature was given a name that means "whale lizard." At first, scientists thought Cetiosaurus was a sea animal, until fossils of the leg bones were found.

WOW! In 1868, a complete Cetiosaurus skeleton was discovered by English paleontologist Sir Richard Owen.

60 ft (9 m)

CETIOSAURUS

▶ A young Cetiosaurus follows its parent across open ground. The adult would protect its young and teach it how to survive.

UNDER ATTACK

WOW!

Scientists
have found 20
Tyrannosaurus
skeletons—more
than of any other
large hunting
dinosaur.

Some dinosaurs lived together in groups called herds. The fully grown adults would join together to protect the youngsters.

Herds of animals work together. If a hunter, such as Tyrannosaurus (tie-rann-oh-saw-rus), threatened to attack a herd of Triceratops (try-ser-ah-tops), they would form a circle.

The adults stood on the outside of the circle with their sharp horns facing outward to protect the youngsters standing on the inside. The Tyrannosaurus would be unable to reach the young, so it would give up the hunt and leave.

▶ Tyrannosaurus cannot break into a circle of defending Triceratops. However, it may return later to try to grab a youngster by surprise.

40 ft (12 m)

TYRANNOSAURUS

▲ A complete fossilized skeleton of Triceratops. Its large horns may have been used to fight other dinosaurs, including hunters.

30 ft
(9 m)

TRICERATOPS

GOING IT ALONE

As a young dinosaur grew older, it would become stronger and begin to learn the skills it needed to survive.

Eventually a youngster would be able to look after itself. Instead of following its parent everywhere, the youngster may gradually start to drift away and begin to live on its own.

Iguanodon (ig-wan-oh-don) fed on shrubs and small trees. A young Iguanodon may stay with its parent for a year or two before it left to live by itself.

DINOSAUR DIG

WHAT	Iguanodon
WHERE	England, Europe
PERIOD	140 million years ago in the early Cretaceous

DIG SITE

▲ An adult Iguanodon jawbone. A youngster would have had a similar jaw and teeth, as it ate the same food.

33 ft (10 m)

IGUANODON

WOW!

Scientists did not realize that dinosaurs had ever existed until fossils of Iguanodon were found in the mid-19th century.

▶ A young Iguanodon tries to keep up with its parent. The adult dinosaur would gradually lose interest in its young as it grew older. Eventually they would separate.

THREAT DISPLAYS

Adults may have been forced to compete with other dinosaurs of the same type.

If there was little food, survival depended on finding good feeding grounds. It is thought that some hunters may have had a home area, or territory, where they would not allow others of their kind to hunt.

Dilophosaurus (die-low-fo-saw-rus) had a pair of bony **crests** growing from the top of its skull. Scientists believe that the dinosaur may have used these crests in a threat display to scare away hunters.

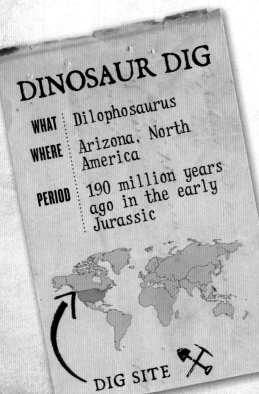

DINOSAUR DIG

WHAT	Dilophosaurus
WHERE	Arizona, North America
PERIOD	190 million years ago in the early Jurassic

DIG SITE

▶ A pair of rival Dilophosaurus display their crests to each other by pacing back and forth. A fight would only take place if neither dinosaur backed down.

▲ This fossil of Dilophosaurus is almost complete, although some of the bones have become mixed up. The crests on its head can clearly be seen.

WOW!

The bones in the crests of Dilophosaurus were as thin as paper in places.

20 ft (6 m)

DILOPHOSAURUS

POWER STRUGGLE

Sometimes threats and displays would not settle a struggle between dinosaurs. They would often fight to decide which was the strongest.

Stegoceras (steg-oh-sair-ass) was a **bonehead** dinosaur. It had a very thick skull with a dome of solid bone on top of its head. Some scientists think that Stegoceras fought each other using their heads.

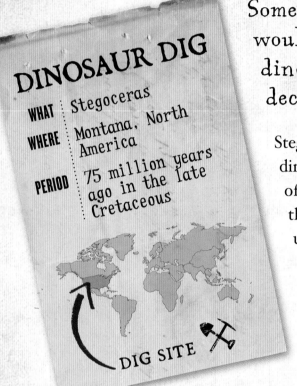

DINOSAUR DIG

WHAT : Stegoceras

WHERE : Montana, North America

PERIOD : 75 million years ago in the late Cretaceous

DIG SITE

▼ Stegoceras fought by charging toward each other. The force used when they crashed together would soon show which dinosaur was the strongest.

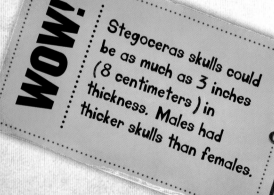

WOW! Stegoceras skulls could be as much as 3 inches (8 centimeters) in thickness. Males had thicker skulls than females.

Stegoceras would run at each other with their heads lowered. They would crash together with enormous force. After a few impacts, the weaker dinosaur would give up the fight. Scientists believe that they probably hit each other on the sides of the body, rather than head-butting.

6.5 ft (2 m)

STEGOCERAS

HERD INSTINCT

Some sauropods, such as Mamenchisaurus (ma-men-key-saw-rus), lived in herds—from as few as 10 dinosaurs to as many as 100.

Living in a herd had advantages because one or two dinosaurs would always be looking out for danger. The dinosaurs could join forces to drive off a hunter. In a herd, plant eaters could find water or good eating grounds more easily.

DINOSAUR DIG

WHAT Mamenchisaurus

WHERE China, Asia

PERIOD 150 million years ago in the late Jurassic

DIG SITE

WOW!

Mamenchisaurus had the longest neck of any dinosaur. It was more than 30 feet (10 meters) in length—that's the same as six people lying end to end.

80 ft (24 m)

MAMENCHISAURUS

▶ A herd of sauropods wanders across a dry plain. Fossil footprints show that younger animals stayed in the center of the herd, where they would be protected from attack.

▶ Mamenchisaurus may have been able to rear up on its back legs, using the tail to balance. Then Mamenchisaurus could feed on even higher leaves on trees.

THE END OF THE STORY

All dinosaurs eventually died. Some were killed by hunters or died after a fight. Others fell victim to disease or to an accident. Some probably just died of old age.

Leaellynasaura (lee-ell-in-ah-saw-rah) lived in Australia. Millions of years ago, the winters would have been very cold. If Leaellynasaura could not keep warm enough, it may have died from the cold.

When a dinosaur died, its body was most likely either to be eaten by the first hunter to find it or to rot away completely. The bones or teeth of only a few creatures remained as fossils.

A dinosaur that died next to a river had a better chance of being fossilized, as its body would have been quickly covered by mud or sand.

DINOSAUR DIG

WHAT Leaellynasaura

WHERE Victoria, Australia

PERIOD 110 million years ago in the mid-Cretaceous

DIG SITE

6.5 ft (2 m)

LEAELLYNASAURA

▶ A dead Leaellynasaura lies beside a frozen river. It is thought that the long, cold winters may have killed off many weaker dinosaurs.

WOW! A large number of bones have been found in Alberta, Canada. Scientists believe that hundreds of dinosaurs were swept away by a fast-flowing river.

FOOD

Did you know that the biggest dinosaurs had the smallest mouths?

Or that some dinosaurs had super-strong jaws to clamp down on their prey?

Read on to discover everything you need to know about hunting and eating...

DINOSAUR SNAPPERS

Some dinosaur hunters were fairly small. They lived by hunting animals that were smaller than themselves.

They had to be able to move quickly and easily to catch their prey. These hunters could leap and change direction suddenly.

Staurikosaurus (store-ick-oh-saw-rus) was a small hunter that ran quickly on its back legs, snapping up food in its mouth. Scientists are not certain to which dinosaur family it belonged.

Eoraptor (ee-oh-rap-tor) probably fed on small animals. It would run quickly after its prey and then tear the victim apart with its small, sharp teeth.

DINOSAUR DIG

WHAT	Eoraptor Staurikosaurus
WHERE	Brazil, South America
PERIOD	225 million years ago in the late Triassic

DIG SITE ⛏

▶ Staurikosaurus would eat anything that it could catch, including large insects.

6.5 ft (2 m)

STAURIKOSAURUS

▼ Eoraptor is the earliest known dinosaur. It may have used its sharp claws to dig for food or to grab smaller animals.

3 ft
(1 m)

EORAPTOR

WOW!

Eoraptor had small teeth, so it probably only hunted small animals.

▶ A scientist cleans an Eoraptor **skull** to remove the surrounding stone. The process can take weeks and needs great care.

LIZARD EATERS

Some early dinosaurs, such as Coelophysis (see-low-fye-sis), hunted lizards and other small animals, including **mammals** and **amphibians**.

The skeleton of Coelophysis was made up of slender, thin bones that were very light. This enabled Coelophysis to move quickly and change direction easily.

The long neck of Coelophysis could twist, so that the head could dart forward to snap up prey. The front legs had clawed hands that were used for digging in soil to find food.

DINOSAUR DIG

WHAT | Coelophysis
WHERE | New Mexico, North America
PERIOD | 225 million years ago in the late Triassic

DIG SITE

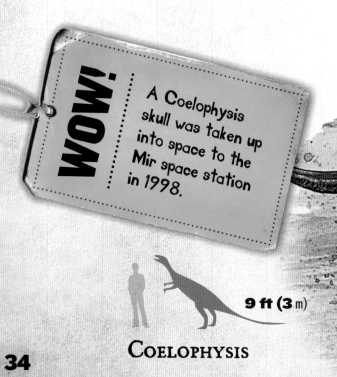

WOW!

A Coelophysis skull was taken up into space to the Mir space station in 1998.

9 ft (3 m)

COELOPHYSIS

▲ A fossil skeleton of Coelophysis. It is very rare to find a complete skeleton with every bone in its place.

▼ Coelophysis gulps down a lizard. Coelophysis would have eaten small prey whole. Larger prey would have been torn apart before being swallowed.

PLANT EATERS

Dinosaurs were a very successful group of animals. They soon took over from other types of reptiles that had ruled the earth up until the Triassic period.

The first dinosaurs were all quite small, but soon larger types began to appear. Plateosaurus (plat-ee-oh-saw-rus) was one of the first big plant eaters, growing up to 26 feet (8 meters) in length, with a heavy body and thick legs.

DINOSAUR DIG

WHAT Plateosaurus

WHERE Germany, Europe

PERIOD 215 million years ago in the late Triassic

DIG SITE

▶ Plateosaurus had jagged, or serrated, teeth that were suited to shredding tough leaves of tree ferns and other large plants of the time.

26 ft (8 m)

PLATEOSAURUS

Plateosaurus walked on all four legs most of the time, but could rear up on its back legs to reach leaves at the top of trees.

The front feet had a large claw on the thumb, which may have been used to dig up roots for Plateosaurus to eat.

WOW!

More than 100 fossilized remains of Plateosaurus have been found in about 50 different locations.

▲ This fossilized skeleton of Plateosaurus has been reconstructed standing upright to show its great size.

STRIPPING LEAVES

Sauropod dinosaurs were the biggest dinosaurs of all, but they had the smallest mouths.

The leaves and shoots that sauropods ate did not provide much energy. As they were so big, sauropods needed to eat huge amounts every day to survive.

It is thought that sauropods did not chew their food at all. They bit off a mouthful of leaves and swallowed them immediately. Sauropods swallowed stones that were moved about by the stomach muscles to mash up the leaves and twigs.

DINOSAUR DIG

WHAT	Brachiosaurus
WHERE	Colorado, North America
PERIOD	150 million years ago in the late Jurassic

DIG SITE

▶ A fossilized skull of Brachiosaurus (brack-ee-oh-saw-rus). The large openings in the skull are for the eyes and nostrils. The huge nostrils may have contained veins carrying blood that could be cooled by the air as it was breathed in.

80 ft (25 m)

BRACHIOSAURUS

WOW!

Sauropods had such long necks that food did not arrive in their stomach until 30 seconds after they swallowed it.

▼ Brachiosaurus prepares to take a mouthful of leaves from a tree. Its long neck allowed Brachiosaurus to eat food that other dinosaurs could not reach.

DESERT DWELLERS

The weather during the early Jurassic period was generally warm and wet.

There may have also been very dry areas, called **deserts**, or long periods of time without rain, called droughts.

DINOSAUR DIG

WHAT	Lufengosaurus
WHERE	Lufeng, China, Asia
PERIOD	200 million years ago in the early Jurassic

DIG SITE

20 ft (6 m)

LUFENGOSAURUS

The animals that lived in these areas had to survive in dry conditions as well as in wet ones. Lufengosaurus (loo-fung-oh-saw-rus) was a plant-eating dinosaur with sharp teeth to shred up tough plant food. The large claws on its front legs helped it to dig for food and water.

The plants were digested in an enormous stomach, which was positioned in front of the back legs. The weight of its stomach meant that Lufengosaurus and similar dinosaurs found it easier to walk on all four legs.

▲ The fossil skeleton of Lufengosaurus has been reconstructed to rear up. This shows how it used its neck to reach high into a tree to find food.

◄ Lufengosaurus could eat tough fernlike plants. Its sharp teeth were ideally suited to this sort of food.

WOW!
Some scientsits believe that the plant eater Jingshanosaurus (yin-shahn-oh-saw-rus) may have also eaten shellfish.

41

WATERY WORLD

All animals need to drink water in order to survive. Water is used to help chemical processes inside the body.

Dinosaurs, like all reptiles, had skin that was covered in tough scales. These scales were waterproof and also kept their body from losing water. Dinosaurs could then store water in their body, so they needed to drink less water than other animals.

DINOSAUR DIG

WHAT	Huayangosaurus
WHERE	China, Asia
PERIOD	165 million years ago in the mid-Jurassic

DIG SITE

13 ft (4 m)

HUAYANGOSAURUS

▶ Huayangosaurus (hoo-ah-yang-oh-saw-rus) drinks from a stream. This dinosaur lived at a time when the climate was warm and wet, so there was always plenty of water to drink.

▼ A fossil skeleton of Huayangosaurus shows the low position of the head. This allowed the dinosaur to feast on shrubs and other low-growing plants.

CLEVER FEEDING

Over time, dinosaurs adapted, or changed, so they could find food successfully. Some were quick, some were huge, and others had specialized body parts.

The plant-eating **ornithopod** had a long, muscular tongue to pull leaves into its mouth. The leaves were then bitten off using the sharp beak at the front of its jaws. Finally, the ornithopod chewed the food using strong teeth at the back of its jaws.

Sauropod dinosaurs were huge plant eaters with a long neck and tail. They weighed up to 80 tons each and ate a huge amount of plant food every day.

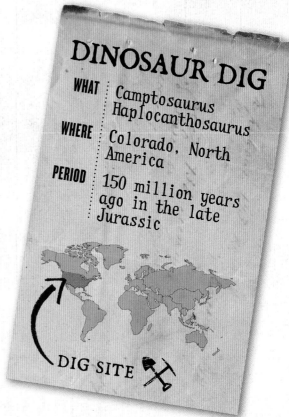

DINOSAUR DIG

WHAT	Camptosaurus Haplocanthosaurus
WHERE	Colorado, North America
PERIOD	150 million years ago in the late Jurassic

DIG SITE

72 ft (22 m)

HAPLOCANTHOSAURUS

◀ Sauropods such as Haplocanthosaurus (hap-low-kan-thoe-saw-rus) used their weight to push over tall trees, so they could reach the leaves at the top.

▲ A fossil skeleton of Camptosaurus (kamp-toe-saw-rus) shows the dinosaur walking on its back legs, although it could also walk on all four.

20 ft (6 m)

CAMPTOSAURUS

▲ Camptosaurus had a skull that was long and low compared to that of other, similar dinosaurs. This allowed space for hundreds of teeth, which were used to chew up food.

THE SOUND OF FOOD

Animals rely on their sense of hearing, especially if they live in dense forests where it is difficult to see for more than a few feet.

Hunters listen out for prey, and plant eaters try to hear if a hunter is nearby. Dinosaur ears were fairly simple. It is thought that they did not have ear flaps. There was probably just a simple hole leading to the inner ear.

WOW!

If a dinosaur put its jaws on the ground, it could "hear" vibrations made by the footsteps of nearby animals.

▶ Allosaurus (al-oh-saw-rus) stops to listen to a sound—it may be prey nearby. Hearing is a key sense for hunting animals and may make the difference between a successful hunt and hunger.

40 ft
(12 m)
ALLOSAURUS

Allosaurus was a large hunter that probably preyed on sauropods, preferring to attack old or weak individuals, as they would be easier to kill.

▲ A fossilized skeleton of Allosaurus. The large, powerful head and strong claws on the front limbs show it was an active hunter.

DINOSAUR DIG

WHAT Allosaurus

WHERE Wyoming, North America

PERIOD 150 million years ago in the late Jurassic

DIG SITE

DESERT DWELLERS

The sense of smell is important to most animals. Plant eaters can smell a hunter from some distance away and may flee before it becomes a danger.

Hunters use scent to track down prey. Also, if the wind is blowing away from the hunter, their victim will not be able to smell them approaching.

The parts of the nose that are used to smell are never fossilized. Therefore, scientists cannot be certain how well dinosaurs could smell. However, some species have long, twisted nostrils that may have contained scent receptors, so these dinosaurs could probably smell better than others.

DINOSAUR DIG

WHAT : Velociraptor

WHERE : Mongolia, Asia

PERIOD : 75 million years ago in the late Cretaceous

DIG SITE

▶ A **pack** of Velociraptor (vel-oss-ee-rap-tor) moves through a Cretaceous forest. There is some evidence that these dinosaurs hunted as a group, working together to find and overcome prey.

▲ This fossilized skull of a Velociraptor shows that this dinosaur had around 80 sharp, curved teeth set in long, narrow jaws. This was ideal for eating meat once prey had been killed.

WOW!
Velociraptor could not bend its tail due to long, thin rods of bones running along it.

6.5 ft (2 m)

VELOCIRAPTOR

IN THE UNDERGROWTH

There were small plant eaters as well as giant sauropods. These dinosaurs may have fed in the undergrowth.

Smaller plant eaters had plenty of food because they could feed on shorter plants that larger dinosaurs missed. They could also hide from danger in the undergrowth.

Micropachycephalosaurus lived among the undergrowth and small plants. They nibbled at leaves and shoots rather than gulping down lots of plant food.

DINOSAUR DIG

WHAT	Micropachy-cephalosaurus
WHERE	Shandong, China, Asia
PERIOD	77 million years ago in the late Cretaceous

DIG SITE

1.5 ft (0.5 m)

MICROPACHYCEPHALOSAURUS

▼ A pair of Micropachycephalosaurus (my-kro-pak-ee-sef-uh-low-saw-rus) feed while looking out for danger. Micropachycephalosaurus may have had striped skin, so they could blend in, or be camouflaged, with the plants.

WOW!

Micropachyceph-alosaurus has the longest name of any dinosaur.

TREE EATERS

Some sauropods had front legs that were much longer than their back legs. They may also have held their neck upright.

The tallest sauropod was Sauroposeidon (saw-roh-pos-eye-don). Its body measured 60 feet (18 meters) in height—as tall as two houses! These dinosaurs used their neck to feed on leaves at the top of conifer trees.

Sauroposeidon was the last sauropod with long front legs. About 95 million years ago, it became extinct.

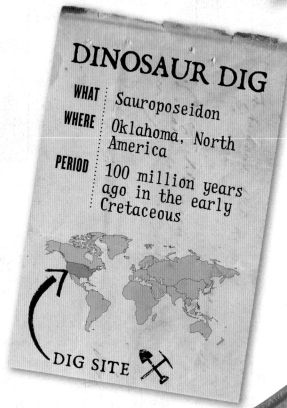

DINOSAUR DIG

WHAT	Sauroposeidon
WHERE	Oklahoma, North America
PERIOD	100 million years ago in the early Cretaceous

DIG SITE

100 ft (30 m)

SAUROPOSEIDON

▶ Sauroposeidon uses its great height to nibble at the top of a conifer tree. Tall trees were out of reach for smaller plant eaters.

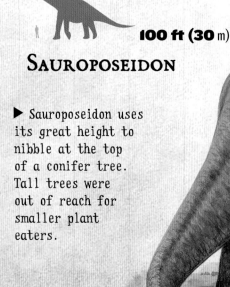

▼ Amargasaurus (ah-mar-gah-saw-rus) was found in Argentina, South America. It may have had flaps of skin connecting the rods of bone that grew up from its neck and back. This was probably used to scare away other dinosaurs.

WOW!

Sauroposeidon was named after the Greek god Poseidon, who was called the "Earth-Shaker," and the earth probably shook when Sauroposeidon moved around.

33 feet (10 m)

AMARGASAURUS

◄ Scientists work to put together a fossilized skeleton of Amargasaurus. Putting the bones into the correct positions is a skilled task.

53

HANDS-ON FEEDING

Some dinosaurs had front legs with special features that were used to help with feeding.

The arms of Deinocheirus (day-no-kye-rus) were 8.5 feet (2.6 meters) in length, with hooked claws on the end that were both sharp and strong.

Some paleontologists think that Deinocheirus used its claws to hook and pull down tree branches so that it could eat the leaves. Others think that it used them to dig in the ground to find roots or insects.

DINOSAUR DIG

WHAT Deinocheirus

WHERE Mongolia, Asia

PERIOD 70 million years ago in the late Cretaceous

DIG SITE

▶ Deinocheirus had the largest arms and claws of any dinosaur. The claws would have been even larger than shown here, as they were covered in horn.

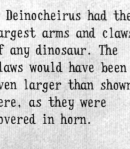

36 ft (11 m)

DEINOCHEIRUS

◀ Some scientists believe that Deinocheirus may have had feathers to keep it warm. Others believe that its skin was actually like that of a reptile.

WOW!

Only the arms of Deinocheirus have been found. Scientists are not quite certain what the rest of its body looked like.

POWERFUL JAWS

The very last group of dinosaurs were the **ceratopsians.** They had unusual teeth and jaws.

Very powerful muscles closed the jaws, while the teeth were arranged to slice food up into tiny pieces before it was swallowed. Scientists think that ceratopsians, such as Leptoceratops (lep-toe-ser-ah-tops), may have feasted on the leaves and twigs of flowering shrubs.

Meat eaters such as Albertosaurus (al-bert-oh-saw-rus) had muscles that could clamp the jaws together with great force, but the muscles that opened the jaws were much weaker.

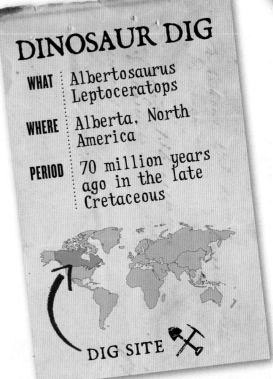

DINOSAUR DIG

WHAT	Albertosaurus Leptoceratops
WHERE	Alberta, North America
PERIOD	70 million years ago in the late Cretaceous

DIG SITE

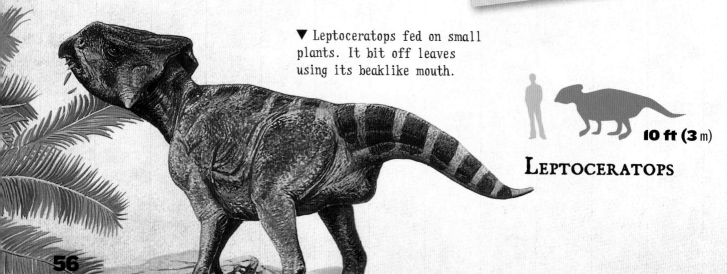

▼ Leptoceratops fed on small plants. It bit off leaves using its beaklike mouth.

10 ft (3 m)

LEPTOCERATOPS

30 ft (9 m)

ALBERTOSAURUS

▲ A fossil skeleton of Albertosaurus is shown with its body bent forward. This gave the dinosaur balance when it walked.

▶ Albertosaurus stands upright to guard its kill— a young ceratopsian dinosaur.

WOW!

In 2000, Philip Currie and his team found 12 Albertosaurus skeletons in Alberta, Canada. This showed that they probably lived and hunted in packs.

A TASTY SNACK

It is usually thought that larger hunters preyed on large plant eaters.

However, even the biggest hunter would have snapped up a much smaller animal if it got the chance. A baby dinosaur or other small creature would have been killed instantly by one bite of the giant jaws.

Scientists think that the big hunters had such strong chemicals in their stomach that they may have been able to digest the bones. Others think that the bones were **regurgitated** from the stomach once the meat had been digested.

DINOSAUR DIG

WHAT : Tarbosaurus

WHERE : Mongolia, Asia

PERIOD : 70 million years ago in the late Cretaceous

DIG SITE

40 ft (12 m)

TARBOSAURUS

▶ The hunter Tarbosaurus (tar-bow-saw-rus) prepares to snap up a young hadrosaur dinosaur. Its long, stabbing teeth and powerful jaws would kill such a small animal with a single bite.

Tarbosaurus was a tyrannosaur that grew to be about 40 feet (12 meters) in length. Like other tyrannosaurs, it had very powerful jaws, but tiny front claws. Some scientists think that Tarbosaurus could not tackle large dinosaurs, so it fed on smaller animals or carrion.

▲ The fossilized head and neck of Tarbosaurus show that this dinosaur had a deep snout and jaws attached to very powerful muscles. Its bite was probably strong enough to crush bones.

WOW!

Tarbosaurus lived in Asia and Tyrannosaurus (tie-rann-oh-saw-rus) in America, but they were very similar. Some scientists believe they were the same animal.

INTO THE FUTURE

Paleontologists believe that birds come from small hunting dinosaurs. They both have feathers, walk on their back legs, and have hollow limb bones.

Some scientists think that the two groups are so similar that they should belong to a single group. They believe that dinosaurs did not become extinct, they just **evolved** to become birds.

DINOSAUR DIG

WHAT Archaeopteryx

WHERE Southern Germany, Europe

PERIOD 155 million years ago in the late Jurassic

DIG SITE

Other scientists point out the differences between the groups. Dinosaurs had teeth, birds do not. Birds can fly, most dinosaurs could not. These scientists think that dinosaurs and birds should continue to be seen as different groups of animals.

◄ This fossilized Archaeopteryx (ark-ee-op-tur-iks) shows the feathers and how they are arranged to form two wings. When this fossil was found, it showed a link between dinosaurs and birds.

1.5 ft (0.5 m)

ARCHAEOPTERYX

◄ Archaeopteryx perches on a tree branch. Scientists think that Archaeopteryx was a good flyer, but only over short distances.

EXPLORING THE AIR

Microraptor (my-krow-rap-tor), meaning "tiny hunter," was named by the scientist who found it because it looked like a small hunting dinosaur.

Then it was noticed that the dinosaur had feathers growing from its arms, legs, and tail. The feathers were long and strong, like those of a modern bird wing. However, its muscles were not strong enough to enable it to fly.

2 ft (60 cm)

MICRORAPTOR

DINOSAUR DIG

WHAT : Microraptor

WHERE : Liaoning, China, Asia

PERIOD : 130 million years ago in the early Cretaceous

DIG SITE

WOW!

In 1999, a man glued the front end of a Microraptor fossil to the back end of a different dinosaur fossil. He then pretended that he had found a new type of dinosaur, but the truth was soon revealed.

It is now thought that Microraptor used its feathers to glide for short distances. It may have lived in forests, where it climbed trees to look for insects to feed on. The tail was probably used to control steering in the air.

◀ Microraptor probably glided from one tree to the next to escape from danger or to pounce on food.

▲ A Microraptor fossil preserved in rock. The feathers can be clearly seen around the bones. Delicate features, such as feathers, are rarely preserved.

HIBERNATION

Although the earth was warmer and wetter during the time of the dinosaurs, there were areas with cooler weather.

Australia and New Zealand lay close to the South Pole about 110 million years ago. During winter, the sun did not shine for weeks on end. The weather was very cold and no plants could grow.

Some of the larger dinosaurs may have walked to warmer areas in winter, but smaller dinosaurs could not escape. Instead, they hibernated.

When an animal hibernates it goes into a very deep sleep. The heart rate and breathing slow down, the body temperature drops, and all bodily functions become slower. During this time, the creature survives on fat stored in its body.

DINOSAUR DIG

WHAT   Leaellynasaura
          Timimus

WHERE Southern Australia

PERIOD 106 million years
          ago in the early
          Cretaceous

DIG SITE

WOW! Scientists did not know that dinosaurs lived in cold parts of the world until the fossil of Leaellynasaura was found in Australia in 1989.

▶ A scene from Australia about 106 million years ago. A group of Timimus (tim-ee-mus) look up at the Southern Lights.

6.5 ft (2 m)

LEAELLYNASAURA

11 ft (3.5 m)

TIMIMUS

SURVIVAL

The ceratopsian dinosaurs became very successful in North America because the plants on which they fed grew everywhere.

DINOSAUR DIG

WHAT : Chasmosaurus Styracosaurus

WHERE : Alberta, North America

PERIOD : 65 million years ago in the late Cretaceous

DIG SITE

All ceratopsians had beaks that they used to crop plant food, and slicing teeth to cut it up before swallowing.

About 65 million years ago, dinosaurs became extinct. It is likely that the plants that plant eaters ate died out, leaving them without any food. Once the plant eaters began to disappear, meat eaters were left with no food either.

▼ Styracosaurus (sty-rak-oh-saw-rus) feeds on plants on the ground. Scientists have found thousands of Styracosaurus fossils, but only one is of a complete skull.

16 ft (5 m)

STYRACOSAURUS

▶ The patterned **neck frill** of Chasmosaurus (kaz-mo-saw-rus) would have been used in threat displays to scare away hunters.

20 ft (6 m)

CHASMOSAURUS

◀ Chasmosaurus had large holes in its neck frill to lighten the weight on its neck.

COMBAT

Did you know that some dinosaurs used their neck frill to look bigger and stronger?

Or that some dinosaurs hunted in packs?

Read on to discover everything you need to know about dinosaurs in combat...

THE HUNTERS

Hunting dinosaurs had many different weapons for attacking their prey, such as teeth and claws.

Some hunters worked alone, but others lived in groups called packs. If a pack of small hunters attacked a larger hunter, the fight would be dramatic.

Herrerasaurus (he-ray-ra-saw-rus) was one of the largest hunters of the late Triassic period. With sharp teeth, it was very ferocious. Herrerasaurus could catch smaller dinosaurs, such as an Eoraptor (ee-oh-rap-tor), with a single bite. If Eoraptors formed a pack, they might stand a chance of survival.

WOW!

Fossils from the Triassic period— the earliest time when the dinosaurs lived— show that the first dinosaurs probably lived in South America.

3 ft (1 m)

EORAPTOR

DINOSAUR DIG

WHAT : Eoraptor
Herrerasaurus

WHERE : Argentina, South America

PERIOD : 225 million years ago in the late Triassic

DIG SITE

◀ A fossilized skull of Herrerasaurus shows the curved-back teeth that helped the dinosaur to grip struggling prey.

10 ft (3 m)

HERRERASAURUS

▼ A pack of Eoraptors attack a much larger Herrerasaurus. The larger dinosaur is more powerful, but a pack of smaller dinosaurs would be able to fight together.

CARRION EATERS

Hunting dinosaurs did not always have to find and kill their prey. Sometimes they found a meal just waiting to be eaten.

A dead body, or **carcass**, that has begun to rot is called **carrion**. Some meat eaters had an extremely good sense of smell and sight to help them to find carrion. They rarely hunted at all. However, even the strongest hunters would feed on carrion if they came across it.

DINOSAUR DIG

WHAT	Dromaeosaurus
WHERE	Canada, North America
PERIOD	75 million years ago in the late Creataceous

DIG SITE

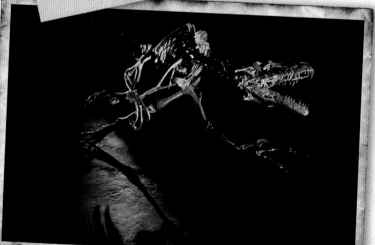

◀ Dromaeosaurus (drom-ee-oh-saw-rus) was equipped with excellent killing weapons: fanglike teeth and very sharp claws.

6.5 ft (2 m)

DROMAEOSAURUS

▼ A group of hunters squabbles over the carcass of a rhynchosaur. Although Dromaeosaurus could easily catch prey, it would also feed on carrion.

73

TAIL SPIKES

Plant-eating dinosaurs needed to be able to protect themselves from hunters in order to survive.

One group of dinosaurs, called **stegosaurs**, developed long, sharp spikes on their tail. Kentrosaurus (ken-troe-saw-rus) was a stegosaur with upright plates of bone along its back, as well as sharp spikes along its tail.

DINOSAUR DIG

WHAT	Allosaurus Kentrosaurus
WHERE	Tanzania, Africa
PERIOD	150 million years ago in the late Jurassic

DIG SITE

If Kentrosaurus faced a large hunter, such as Allosaurus (al-oh-saw-rus), it would easily be defeated. The only chance Kentrosaurus had of surviving was to hit Allosaurus with its tail spikes. This would injure the hunter and Kentrosaurus could escape.

16.5 ft (5 m)

KENTROSAURUS

▶ Allosaurus attacks Kentrosaurus. The hunter is more than twice as large, so Kentrosaurus has to use all its power to escape from Allosaurus.

◀ A fossil skeleton of Allosaurus shows how it might stride forward while hunting. The head could lunge out to bite prey.

40 ft (12 m)

ALLOSAURUS

WOW!

The bone spikes of Kentrosaurus would have been covered in shiny horn with extremely sharp points, making them excellent weapons.

DINOSAUR RUNNERS

Dinosaurs could run well. This skill was important for chasing prey and escaping from danger.

As their legs grew straight down from the hips, dinosaurs only needed to move their legs in order to walk or run. Other reptiles need to swing their body from side to side because their legs grow out from the sides. Therefore, dinosaurs could move faster while using less energy than many other reptiles.

Coelophysis (see-low-fye-sis) was an early hunting dinosaur. It ran on its back legs. Coelophysis was fast and agile enough to snap up other, smaller animals of the time. It was also able to flee quickly from danger.

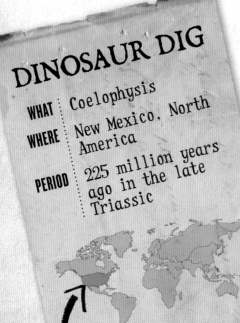

DINOSAUR DIG

WHAT	Coelophysis
WHERE	New Mexico, North America
PERIOD	225 million years ago in the late Triassic

DIG SITE

▶ Dinosaurs and other animals flee as fire sweeps across the Triassic landscape of North America. Events such as this have been recorded in the fossil record—a list of all the fossils ever discovered.

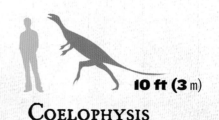

10 ft (3 m)

COELOPHYSIS

◀ A fossil skeleton of Coelophysis. The remains of its last meal have been preserved inside its stomach.

WOW! There are two dinosaur groups. The ornithischians had hips like modern birds, and the saurischians had hips like modern lizards.

THE CHASE

Some smaller plant eaters relied on speed to escape from danger.

They had no weapons and were fairly weak, so they would run away as soon as they saw a hunter. However, many meat eaters were also able to run very quickly, so they would chase the smaller dinosaur.

If a plant eater, such as Hypsilophodon (hip-see-loff-oh-don), could run faster than a hunter, such as Deinonychus (die-non-ee-kuss), it would escape. If it could not, then it would fall victim and end up as a meal for the hunter.

DINOSAUR DIG

WHAT	Deinonychus Hypsilophodon
WHERE	Montana, North America
PERIOD	100 million years ago in the early Cretaceous

DIG SITE

8 ft (2.5 m)

HYPSILOPHODON

◄ The skull of a Deinonychus shows that its teeth were very sharp and curved backward. This helped it to bite into the prey's flesh and hold on tightly during a struggle.

10 ft (3 m)

DEINONYCHUS

▶ If Deinonychus attacked a herd of Hypsilophodon, they would panic and spread out. One of them would be slower than the rest and would easily be injured by the sharp claws of Deinonychus.

WOW!

It is believed that some dinosaurs could run as fast as the swiftest modern animals— up to 40 miles (60 kilometers) an hour.

HUNTING ALONE

A hunter working alone would have avoided attacking a large plant eater.

It would have been difficult for meat eaters, such as Ceratosaurus (se-rat-oh-saw-rus), to attack Brachiosaurus (brack-ee-oh-saw-rus) because it was so large. Although Brachiosaurus had no weapons such as sharp teeth or claws, it could stamp or kick with great force. Ceratosaurus would need to take Brachiosaurus by surprise, or be very lucky, to win the combat.

▲ This famous skeleton of a Brachiosaurus from a museum in Berlin, Germany, is the largest mounted dinosaur skeleton in the world. The fossilized skeleton had several bones missing, which were replaced with fossil bones taken from other, similar dinosaurs.

80 ft (25 m)

BRACHIOSAURUS

DINOSAUR DIG

WHAT	Brachiosaurus Ceratosaurus
WHERE	Wyoming, North America
PERIOD	150 million years ago in the late Jurassic

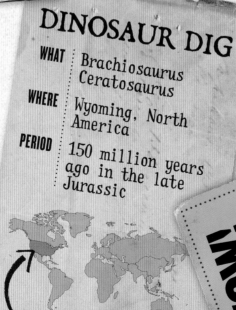

DIG SITE ⚒

WOW! Brachiosaurus had nostrils on top of its head. This enabled the dinosaur to make a noise that may have been used to communicate with other dinosaurs.

20 ft (6 m)

CERATOSAURUS

▼ Ceratosaurus prepares to attack an adult Brachiosaurus. Hunters would probably have preferred to avoid such large individuals and would attack younger animals instead.

EASY PREY

Most hunters preferred to find an easier meal than fighting a fully grown sauropod. Young sauropods were easier to kill.

Young dinosaurs were smaller and weaker than adults, and they had less experience of how to fight or escape from danger.

Megalosaurus (meg-ah-low-saw-rus) was armed with sharp teeth in strong jaws, and had powerful claws on its feet. If it could catch a dinosaur smaller than itself, it would have an easy meal. Old or sick animals were also easier to overcome than healthy adults.

DINOSAUR DIG

WHAT | Megalosaurus
WHERE | France, Europe
PERIOD | 165 million years ago in the mid-Jurassic

DIG SITE

▶ Megalosaurus prepares to eat a young sauropod that it has killed. It was the most powerful hunter in Europe during the late Jurassic Period.

30 ft (9 m)

MEGALOSAURUS

▲ The teeth of Megalosaurus were very sharp and curved backward. This would give the dinosaur a firm grip on struggling prey.

WOW! Fossilized sauropod bones have been found covered in scratch and bite marks—probably from the teeth of hunting dinosaurs!

FATAL WOUNDS

Deinonychus (die-non-ee-kuss) belonged to a group of ferocious hunters known as **raptors.**

These fast-moving hunters had a large, curved claw on each of their back legs. This weapon was held off the ground so that it stayed sharp and ready for action.

▶ A pack of Deinonychus attack Tenontosaurus. Scientists have found a fossil showing that Tenontosaurus had once been killed by a group of these hunters.

▲ This skeleton shows Deinonychus leaping forward as though it were about to attack a victim.

DINOSAUR DIG

WHAT	Deinonychus Tenontosaurus
WHERE	Wyoming, North America
PERIOD	100 million years ago in the early Cretaceous

DIG SITE ⚒

A group of Deinonychus may have pounced on a larger dinosaur and used their back claws to cause deep wounds. Then they would run off before Tenontosaurus (ten-on-toe-saw-rus) could fight back. They would probably wait for their prey to bleed to death, then move in to feast on the body.

WOW!

Some scientists believe that Deinonychus may have been covered in feathers, but others think that its skin was scaly.

10 ft (3 m)

DEINONYCHUS

23 ft (7 m)

TENONTOSAURUS

A GAME OF BLUFF

When they meet a dangerous hunter or rival, many animals will try to make themselves look bigger and stronger than they really are. They hope that this will frighten off the other animal.

Many scientists think that ceratopsian dinosaurs used their neck frill as a **bluffing** weapon. The frill looked large and impressive. The animal would lift up its frill so that it looked as big as possible, then move it from side to side. It was actually made of a thin layer of bone and skin. The frill may also have been used to attract females before mating.

DINOSAUR DIG

WHAT Monoclonius

WHERE Montana, North America

PERIOD 75 million years ago in the late Creataceous

DIG SITE

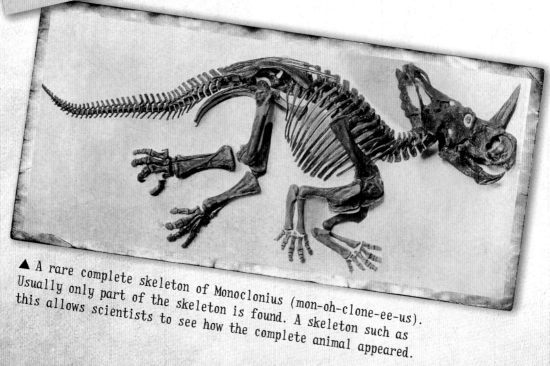

▲ A rare complete skeleton of Monoclonius (mon-oh-clone-ee-us). Usually only part of the skeleton is found. A skeleton such as this allows scientists to see how the complete animal appeared.

16.5 ft (5 m)

MONOCLONIUS

▶ Monoclonius lowers its head and stamps on the ground with its front feet as it prepares for a fight. Combats may have been between rivals of the same species, or against hunters.

THE AMBUSH

Tarbosaurus (tar-bow-saw-rus) was a large, powerful hunter. It had long, sharp teeth set in jaws that were powered by very strong muscles.

However, it was unable to run very quickly. The best chance it had of killing prey was to ambush it. Tarbosaurus would wait in bushes or behind trees, then leap out on a victim.

Scientists know a lot about Tarbosaurus because they have found many fossilized skeletons. Few other dinosaurs from Asia have been found in such numbers, so there must have been many of them around in the late Cretaceous period.

DINOSAUR DIG

WHAT : Tarbosaurus
WHERE : Mongolia, Asia
PERIOD : 80 million years ago in the late Creataceous

DIG SITE

36 ft (12 m)

TARBOSAURUS

▲ The teeth of Tarbosaurus were smaller than those of its close relative Tyrannosaurus (tie-rann-oh-saw-rus).

▲ The mouth of Tarbosaurus could be opened very wide to reveal its fangs. The wide **gape** and strong jaws show that it may have killed prey by running at them with its mouth open.

¡WOW!

The tiny arms of Tarbosaurus were too small to reach its mouth, so scientists are not sure what they were for.

ALARM!

Plant eaters that live in herds or flocks usually have a way of warning others if danger threatens.

Some animals will call loudly or stamp their feet on the ground to make a noise. Others have brightly colored parts of their body that they will reveal suddenly, flashing a patch of color on and off.

DINOSAUR DIG

WHAT Anserimimus
Oviraptor
Protoceratops
Tarbosaurus

WHERE Mongolia, Asia

PERIOD 75 million years ago in the late Cretaceous

DIG SITE

6.5 ft (2 m)

OVIRAPTOR

6.5 ft (2 m)

PROTOCERATOPS

▼ A pair of Protoceratops (pro-toe-ser-ah-tops) guard their nest.

Some dinosaurs had brightly colored feathers growing from their tail. These may have been used as an alarm signal. The dinosaur would show the back of the fan as it fled from danger. Other dinosaurs would follow because they knew that they would also be running away from the hunting dinosaur.

11 ft (3 m)

ANSERIMIMUS

40 ft (12 m)

TARBOSAURUS

◀ A tyrannosaur chases Anserimimus (ann-sair-ee-me-mus) and Oviraptor (oh-vee-rap-tor).

WOW!
A pack of hunters sometimes ambushed prey. One hunter would allow itself to be seen, so that the prey ran away—straight toward the other hunters.

WEAPONS

When a hunter attacked prey, it would try to avoid any weapons that the plant eater had. The plant eater would do its best to use those weapons to defend itself.

Triceratops (try-ser-ah-tops) had three long, sharp horns on its head to defend itself against hunters. When Tyrannosaurus (tie-rann-oh-saw-rus) attacked, Triceratops would stab the hunter. If Tyrannosaurus became injured, then Triceratops would be able to escape.

DINOSAUR DIG

WHAT : Triceratops
Tyrannosaurus

WHERE : Alberta, North America

PERIOD : 70 million years ago in the late Cretaceous

DIG SITE

▶ A skeleton of Tyrannosaurus shows how it would lunge forward to attack its prey.

40 ft (12 m)

TYRANNOSAURUS

30 ft (9 m)

TRICERATOPS

If Tyrannosaurus could only make one good bite, it may have stood back to wait for the plant eater to become weak through loss of blood. Then it would move in to make the kill.

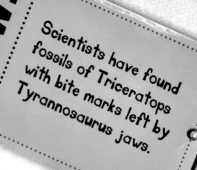

WOW!

Scientists have found fossils of Triceratops with bite marks left by Tyrannosaurus jaws.

▼ Tyrannosaurus battles with Triceratops by trying to bite into the soft sides of the plant eater while avoiding its sharp horns.

THE TAIL CLUB

The armored dinosaurs, or **ankylosaurs,** had a unique way of defending themselves from attack.

The back, sides, head, and tail of Pinacosaurus (pin-ah-coe-saw-rus) had a thick armor of bone covered in horn. Pinacosaurus also had a heavy bone tail club, which it would use to stop an attacker, such as Tarbosaurus (tar-bow-saw-rus), from flipping it over. A blow from the club could seriously injure a hunter.

DINOSAUR DIG

WHAT	Pinacosaurus Tarbosaurus
WHERE	Mongolia, Asia
PERIOD	80 million years ago in the late Cretaceous

DIG SITE

WOW!

Ankylosaurs have been found all over the world, except in Africa.

18 ft (5.5 m)

PINACOSAURUS

◀ The fossilized skeleton of an ankylosaur. Many skeletons are found with the bones scattered, so they need to be put back in position to show what the dinosaur looked like.

40 ft (12 m)

TARBOSAURUS

▼ Tarbosaurus is knocked over by a hit from the tail of Pinacosaurus. To make a successful attack, Tarbosaurus had to turn the armored dinosaur over and attack its soft belly.

HEAD TO HEAD

If a hunting dinosaur was extremely hungry, it may have risked an attack on a plant eater that was ready to defend itself.

Tyrannosaurus (tie-rann-oh-saw-rus) was a powerful killer and may sometimes have become desperate enough to attack an equally strong victim.

Styracosaurus (sty-rak-oh-saw-rus) had a huge, sharp horn growing from its nose, which could cause a serious wound to Tyrannosaurus.

WOW!

One fossil of Styracosaurus was found covered in charcoal. This showed that it had probably died in a forest fire.

DINOSAUR DIG

WHAT : Styracosaurus
Tyrannosaurus

WHERE : Montana, North America

PERIOD : 70 million years ago in the late Cretaceous

DIG SITE

16.5 ft (5 m)

STYRACOSAURUS

▲ The teeth of Tyrannosaurus were only lightly fixed to the jaw and often broke off, so Tyrannosaurus constantly grew new teeth.

40 ft (12 m)

TYRANNOSAURUS

▼ These two hungry tyrannosaurs are searching for another Styracosaurus to attack.

FINAL BATTLE

As conditions changed, new types of dinosaurs gradually evolved and older types died out.

Sauropods became much rarer and stegosaurs died out completely. They were replaced by ceratopsians and hadrosaurs.

Suddenly, about 65 million years ago, all the dinosaurs became extinct. Many other types of animals died out at the same time.

Scientists are not certain what caused this mass extinction. Some think that a meteorite hit the earth, wiping out huge numbers of animals. Others think that a sudden change in climate caused the deaths.

DINOSAUR DIG

WHAT : Triceratops Tyrannosaurus

WHERE : Colorado, North America

PERIOD : 65 million years ago in the late Cretaceous

DIG SITE

WOW!

When the first dinosaur fossils were found, people thought that they were the bones of giant men.

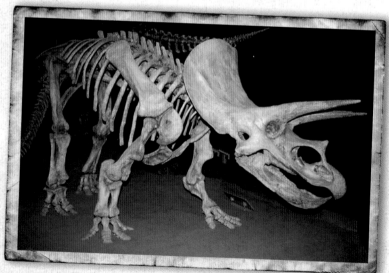

▲ This skeleton of Triceratops (try-ser-ah-tops) shows both the long, sharp horns and the large neck frill. It was a sturdy, powerful animal.

▼ Triceratops prepares to face Tyrannosaurus (tie-rann-oh-saw-rus) in battle. Tyrannosaurus would have tried to avoid the sharp horns of its prey.

30 ft (9 m)

TRICERATOPS

40 ft (12 m)

TYRANNOSAURUS

DINO GUIDE

For every dinosaur in this book and many more, learn how to pronounce their name, find out their length and weight, and discover what they ate.

Coelophysis

PRONUNCIATION
see-low-fye-sis
LENGTH 10 feet (3 meters)
WEIGHT 75-80 pounds (35 kilograms)
DIET Small animals

Efraasia

PRONUNCIATION
ef-rah-see-ah
LENGTH 23 feet (7 meters)
WEIGHT 1,300 pounds (600 kilograms)
DIET Plants

Eoraptor

PRONUNCIATION
ee-oh-rap-tor
LENGTH 3 feet (1 meter)
WEIGHT 7-30 pounds (3-15 kilograms)
DIET Small animals

Herrerasaurus

PRONUNCIATION
he-ray-ra-saw-rus
LENGTH 10 feet (3 meters)
WEIGHT 450 pounds (200 kilograms)
DIET Animals

Melanorosaurus

PRONUNCIATION
mel-an-or-oh-saw-rus
LENGTH 33 feet (10 meters)
WEIGHT 1 ton
DIET Plants

Mussaurus

PRONUNCIATION
muss-saw-rus
LENGTH 13 feet (4 meters)
WEIGHT 330 pounds (150 kilograms)
DIET Plants

Pisanosaurus

PRONUNCIATION
peez-an-oh-saw-rus
LENGTH 3 feet (1 meter)
WEIGHT 6.5 pounds (3 kilograms)
DIET Plants

Plateosaurus

PRONUNCIATION
plat-ee-oh-saw-rus
LENGTH 26 feet (8 meters)
WEIGHT 1 ton
DIET Plants

Procompsognathus

PRONUNCIATION
pró-comp-sog-nay-thus
LENGTH 4 feet (1.3 meters)
WEIGHT 4.5-7 pounds (2-3 kilograms)
DIET Small animals

Riojasaurus

PRONUNCIATION
ree-oh-ha-saw-rus
LENGTH 33 feet (10 meters)
WEIGHT 1 ton
DIET Plants

Saltopus

PRONUNCIATION
sall-toe-puss
LENGTH Less than 3 feet (1 meter)
WEIGHT 2-4.5 pounds (1-2 kilograms)
DIET Small animals

Staurikosaurus

PRONUNCIATION
store-ick-oh-saw-rus
LENGTH 6.5 feet (2 meters)
WEIGHT 65 pounds (30 kilograms)
DIET Small animals

Allosaurus

PRONUNCIATION

al-oh-saw-rus

LENGTH 40 feet (12 meters)

WEIGHT 1.5-2 tons

DIET Animals

Anchisaurus

PRONUNCIATION

an-kee-saw-rus

LENGTH 8 feet (2.5 meters)

WEIGHT 75 pounds (35 kilograms)

DIET Plants

Apatosaurus

PRONUNCIATION

ap-at-oh-saw-rus

LENGTH 80 feet (25 meters)

WEIGHT 25-35 tons

DIET Plants

Archaeopteryx

PRONUNCIATION

ark-ee-op-tur-iks

LENGTH 1.5 feet (0.5 meters)

WEIGHT 1 pound (0.5 kilograms)

DIET Animals

Brachiosaurus

PRONUNCIATION

brack-ee-oh-saw-rus

LENGTH 80 feet (25 meters)

WEIGHT 50 tons

DIET Plants

Camptosaurus

PRONUNCIATION

kamp-toe-saw-rus

LENGTH 20 feet (6 meters)

WEIGHT 1-2 tons

DIET Plants

Ceratosaurus

PRONUNCIATION

se-rat-oh-saw-rus

LENGTH 20 feet (6 meters)

WEIGHT 1,500-2,000 pounds (700-850 kilograms)

DIET Animals

Cetiosaurus
PRONUNCIATION
set-ee-oh-saw-rus
LENGTH 60 feet (18 meters)
WEIGHT 15-20 tons
DIET Plants

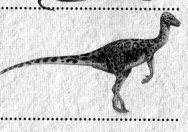

Coelurus
PRONUNCIATION
seel-yur-rus
LENGTH 7 feet (2 meters)
WEIGHT 33 pounds (15 kilograms)
DIET Animals

Compsognathus
PRONUNCIATION
comp-sog-nay-thus
LENGTH 3-5 feet (1-1.5 meters)
WEIGHT 6 pounds (3 kilograms)
DIET Small animals

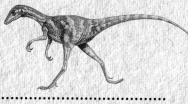

Dicraeosaurus
PRONUNCIATION
die-kree-oh-saw-rus
LENGTH 42-65 feet (13-20 meters)
WEIGHT 10 tons
DIET Plants

Dilophosaurus
PRONUNCIATION
die-low-fo-saw-rus
LENGTH 20 feet (6 meters)
WEIGHT 880 pounds (400 kilograms)
DIET Animals

Euhelopus
PRONUNCIATION
you-hel-oh-puss
LENGTH 32-49 feet (10-15 meters)
WEIGHT 10-25 tons
DIET Plants

Haplocanthosaurus
PRONUNCIATION
hap-low-kan-thoe-saw-rus
LENGTH 72 feet (22 meters)
WEIGHT 20 tons
DIET Plants

Huayangosaurus

PRONUNCIATION

hoo-ah-yang-oh-saw-rus

LENGTH 13 feet (4 meters)

WEIGHT 880-1,300 pounds (400-600 kilograms)

DIET Plants

Jingshanosaurus

PRONUNCIATION

yin-shahn-oh-saw-rus

LENGTH 25 feet (7.5 meters)

WEIGHT 1 ton

DIET Plants

Kentrosaurus

PRONUNCIATION

ken-troe-saw-rus

LENGTH 16.5 feet (5 meters)

WEIGHT 2 tons

DIET Plants

Lesothosaurus

PRONUNCIATION

le-so-toe-saw-rus

LENGTH 3 feet (1 meter)

WEIGHT 4-7 pounds (2-3 kilograms)

DIET Plants

Lufengosaurus

PRONUNCIATION

loo-fung-oh-saw-rus

LENGTH 20 feet (6 meters)

WEIGHT 500 pounds (220 kilograms)

DIET Plants

Mamenchisaurus

PRONUNCIATION

ma-men-key-saw-rus

LENGTH 80 feet (24 meters)

WEIGHT 12-15 tons

DIET Plants

JURASSIC PERIOD
206 to 145
MILLION YEARS AGO

Megalosaurus
PRONUNCIATION
meg-ah-low-saw-rus
LENGTH 30 feet (9 meters)
WEIGHT 1 ton
DIET Plants

Ornitholestes
PRONUNCIATION
or-nith-oh-less-teez
LENGTH 6.5 feet (2 meters)
WEIGHT 65 pounds (30 kilograms)
DIET Animals

Sinosauropteryx
PRONUNCIATION
sy-no-saw-op-tur-iks
LENGTH 3 feet (1 meter)
WEIGHT 6.5 pounds (3 kilograms)
DIET Small animals

Stegosaurus
PRONUNCIATION
steg-oh-saw-rus
LENGTH 26-30 feet (8-9 meters)
WEIGHT 2-3 tons
DIET Plants

Supersaurus
PRONUNCIATION
soo-per-saw-rus
LENGTH 100-130 feet (30-40 meters)
WEIGHT 30-50 tons
DIET Plants

Albertosaurus

PRONUNCIATION
al-bert-oh-saw-rus
LENGTH 30 feet (9 meters)
WEIGHT 2.5 tons
DIET Animals

Amargasaurus

PRONUNCIATION
ah-mar-gah-saw-rus
LENGTH 33 feet (10 meters)
WEIGHT 5-7 tons
DIET Plants

Anserimimus

PRONUNCIATION
ann-sair-ee-me-mus
LENGTH 10 feet (3 meters)
WEIGHT 650 pounds (300 kilograms)
DIET Small animals

Centrosaurus

PRONUNCIATION
sen-tro-saw-rus
LENGTH 20 feet (6 meters)
WEIGHT 3 tons
DIET Plants

Chasmosaurus

PRONUNCIATION
kaz-mo-saw-rus
LENGTH 20 feet (6 meters)
WEIGHT 2-3 tons
DIET Plants

Deinocheirus

PRONUNCIATION
day-no-kye-rus
LENGTH 36 feet (11 meters)
WEIGHT 4-7 tons
DIET Animals and plants

Deinonychus

PRONUNCIATION
die-non-ee-kuss
LENGTH 10 feet (3 meters)
WEIGHT 130 pounds (60 kilograms)
DIET Small animals

Dromaeosaurus

PRONUNCIATION
drom-ee-oh-saw-rus
LENGTH 6.5 feet (2 meters)
WEIGHT 55 pounds (25 kilograms)
DIET Animals

Euoplocephalus

PRONUNCIATION
you-oh-ploe-sef-ah-lus
LENGTH 20-23 feet (6-7 meters)
WEIGHT 2 tons
DIET Plants

Hypsilophodon

PRONUNCIATION
hip-see-loff-oh-don
LENGTH 8 feet (2.5 meters)
WEIGHT 45-90 pounds (20-40 kilograms)
DIET Plants

Iguanodon

PRONUNCIATION
ig-wan-oh-don
LENGTH 33 feet (10 meters)
WEIGHT 4-5 tons
DIET Plants

Jobaria

PRONUNCIATION
joe-barr-ee-ah
LENGTH 65 feet (20 meters)
WEIGHT 18-20 tons
DIET Plants

Leaellynasaura

PRONUNCIATION
lee-ell-in-ah-saw-rah
LENGTH 6.5 feet (2 meters)
WEIGHT 22 pounds (10 kilograms)
DIET Plants

Leptoceratops

PRONUNCIATION
lep-toe-ser-ah-tops
LENGTH 10 feet (3 meters)
WEIGHT 100-450 pounds (50-200 kilograms)
DIET Plants

Maiasaura

PRONUNCIATION
my-yah-saw-rah
LENGTH 30 feet (9 meters)
WEIGHT 3-4 tons
DIET Plants

Micropachycephalosaurus

PRONUNCIATION
my-kro-pak-ee-sef-uh-low-saw-rus
LENGTH 1.5 feet (0.5 meters)
WEIGHT 45 pounds (20 kilograms)
DIET Plants

Microraptor

PRONUNCIATION
my-krow-rap-tor
LENGTH 2 feet (60 centimeters)
WEIGHT 2 pounds (1 kilogram)
DIET Small animals

Monoclonius

PRONUNCIATION
mon-oh-clone-ee-us
LENGTH 16.5 feet (5 meters)
WEIGHT 2-3 tons
DIET Plants

Oviraptor

PRONUNCIATION
oh-vee-rap-tor
LENGTH 6.5 feet (2 meters)
WEIGHT 65 pounds (30 kilograms)
DIET Small animals and plants

Pinacosaurus
PRONUNCIATION
pin-ah-coe-saw-rus
LENGTH 18 feet (5.5 meters)
WEIGHT 1-2 tons
DIET Plants

Protoceratops
PRONUNCIATION
pro-toe-ser-ah-tops
LENGTH 6.5 feet (2 meters)
WEIGHT 330-550 pounds (150-250 kilograms)
DIET Plants

Sauroposeidon
PRONUNCIATION
saw-roh-pos-eye-don
LENGTH 100 feet (30 meters)
WEIGHT 50-80 tons
DIET Plants

Stegoceras
PRONUNCIATION
steg-oh-sair-ass
LENGTH 6.5 feet (2 meters)
WEIGHT 110-150 pounds (50-70 kilograms)
DIET Plants

Stygimoloch
PRONUNCIATION
stij-ee-mol-ock
LENGTH 6.5-10 feet (2-3 meters)
WEIGHT 150-450 pounds (70-200 kilograms)
DIET Plants

Styracosaurus
PRONUNCIATION
sty-rak-oh-saw-rus
LENGTH 16 feet (5 meters)
WEIGHT 3 tons
DIET Plants

Tarbosaurus
PRONUNCIATION
tar-bow-saw-rus
LENGTH 40 feet (12 meters)
WEIGHT 4 tons
DIET Large animals

Tenontosaurus
PRONUNCIATION
ten-on-toe-saw-rus
LENGTH 23 feet (7 meters)
WEIGHT 1 ton
DIET Plants

Timimus
PRONUNCIATION
tim-ee-mus
LENGTH 11 feet (3.5 meters)
WEIGHT 650 pounds (300 kilograms)
DIET Unknown

Triceratops
PRONUNCIATION
try-ser-ah-tops
LENGTH 30 feet (9 meters)
WEIGHT 5-8 tons
DIET Plants

Tyrannosaurus
PRONUNCIATION
tie-rann-oh-saw-rus
LENGTH 40 feet (12 meters)
WEIGHT 6 tons
DIET Large animals

Velociraptor
PRONUNCIATION
vel-oss-ee-rap-tor
LENGTH 6.5 feet (2 meters)
WEIGHT 45-65 pounds (20-30 kilograms)
DIET Small animals

GLOSSARY

Adult
An animal that is fully grown.

Amphibian
An animal that lays its eggs in water, but lives most of its life on land.

Ankylosaur
A type of dinosaur that had armor across its back and other parts of its body.

Bluff
To deceive.

Bonehead
A type of dinosaur that had a thick layer of bone on top of its skull.

Carcass
The body of a dead animal.

Carrion
Meat from a dead animal that the hunter has not killed itself.

Ceratopsian
A group of dinosaurs that had a neck frill and teeth designed for slicing. Most ceratopsians also had horns on their head.

Crest
Bone on the top of the head.

Cretaceous
The third period of time in the age of the dinosaurs. The Cretaceous began about 145 million years ago and ended about 65 million years ago.

Desert
A very dry area of land where few, if any, plants or animals live.

Dinosaur
A type of reptile that lived millions of years ago. All dinosaurs are now extinct.

Evolve
To develop gradually over a long period of time.

Extinct
Not existing any more. An animal is extinct when they have all died out.

Fossil
Any part of a plant or animal that has been preserved in rock. Also traces of plants or animals, such as footprints.

Gape
To open the mouth wide.

Hatch
To emerge from an egg.

Herd
A group of animals that live together.

Jurassic
The second period of time in the age of the dinosaurs. The Jurassic began about 206 million years ago and ended about 145 million years ago.

Mammal
An animal that has hair or fur and produces milk for its babies.

Neck frill
A thin plate of bone and skin growing from the back of an animal's skull.

Nursery
A place where dinosaurs went to hatch their babies and where the young lived for some time afterward.

Ornithopod
A group of plant-eating dinosaurs that had a beak and strong chewing teeth.

Pack
A group of hunting animals.

Paleontologist
A scientist who studies ancient forms of life, including dinosaurs.

Raptor
A type of dinosaur that had a very large claw on each of its back legs.

Regurgitate
To bring swallowed food up from the stomach into the mouth.

Reptile
A cold-blooded animal, such as a lizard. Dinosaurs were reptiles.

Sauropod
A type of dinosaur that had a long neck and tail. Sauropods included the largest of all dinosaurs.

Skeleton
The bones in an animal's body.

Skull
The bones of the head of an animal. The skull does not include the jaw, but many skulls have jaws attached.

Stegosaur
A type of dinosaur that had upright plates or spikes growing from its back.

Triassic
The first period of time in the age of the dinosaurs. The Triassic began about 248 million years ago and ended about 208 million years ago.

Undergrowth
Bushes, small trees, and other plants that grow under bigger plants and trees.

INDEX

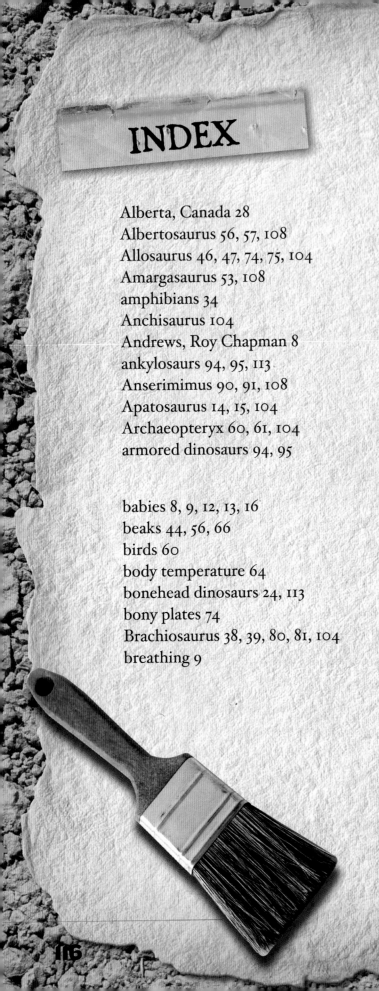

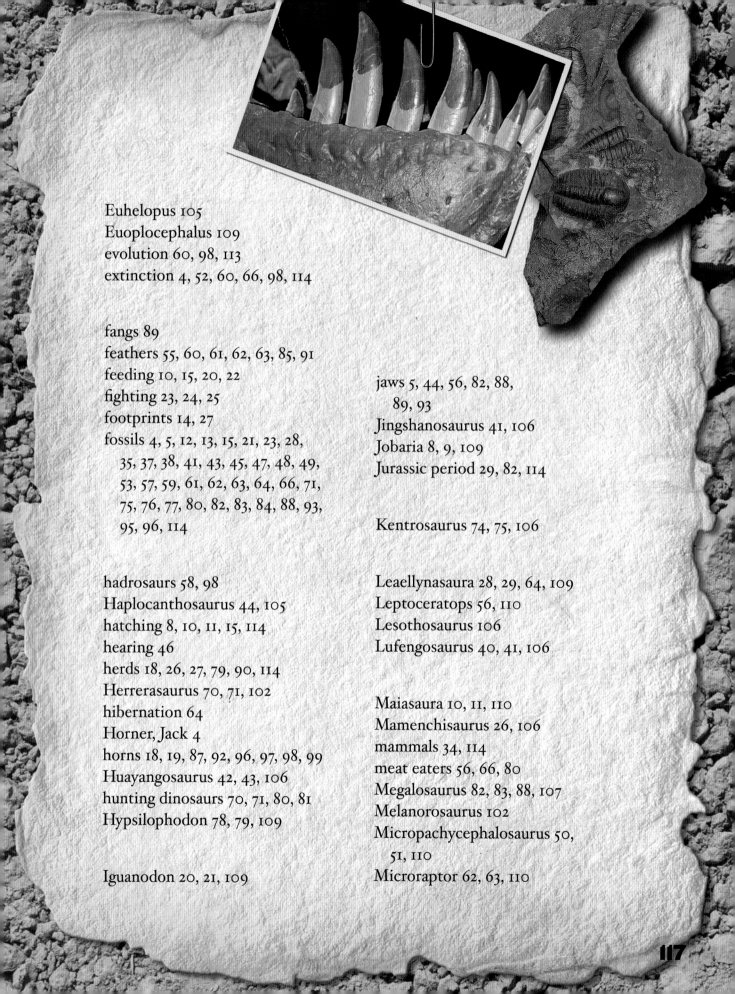

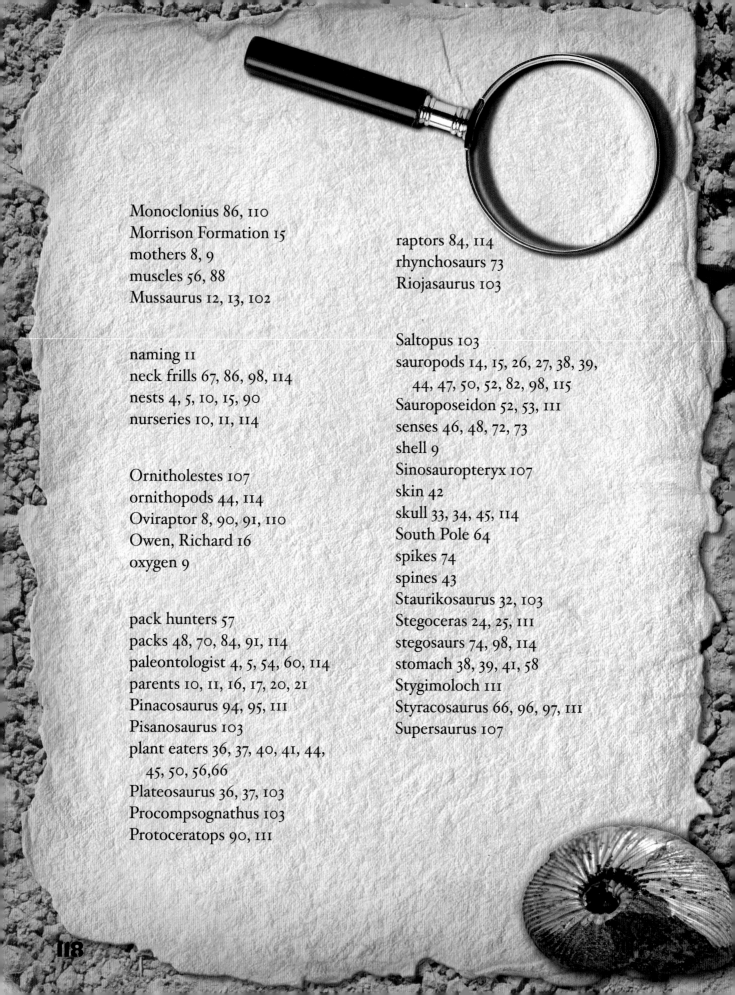

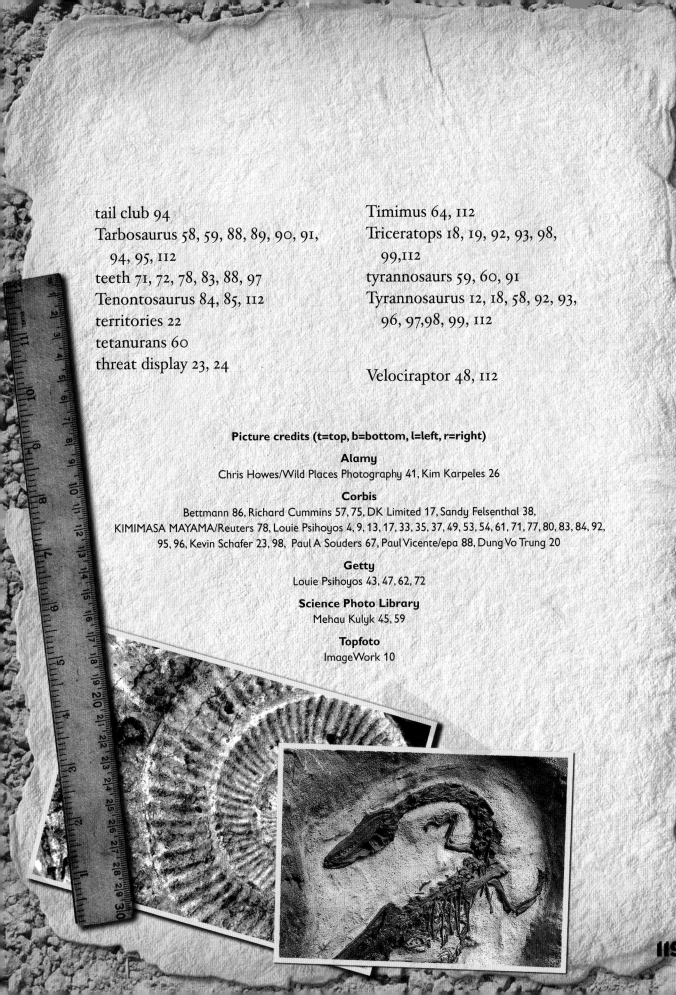

Picture credits (t=top, b=bottom, l=left, r=right)

Alamy
Chris Howes/Wild Places Photography 41, Kim Karpeles 26

Corbis
Bettmann 86, Richard Cummins 57, 75, DK Limited 17, Sandy Felsenthal 38,
KIMIMASA MAYAMA/Reuters 78, Louie Psihoyos 4, 9, 13, 17, 33, 35, 37, 49, 53, 54, 61, 71, 77, 80, 83, 84, 92,
95, 96, Kevin Schafer 23, 98, Paul A Souders 67, Paul Vicente/epa 88, Dung Vo Trung 20

Getty
Louie Psihoyos 43, 47, 62, 72

Science Photo Library
Mehau Kulyk 45, 59

Topfoto
ImageWork 10

Copyright © QEB
Publishing 2014

Published in the United States
by QEB Publishing, Inc.
3 Wrigley, Suite A
Irvine, CA 92618

www.qed-publishing.co.uk

Library of Congress Control Numbers:
2008011533, 2008011534, 2008011535, 2008011571

ISBN 978 1 60992 702 8

Printed in China

Author Rupert Matthews
Consultant Neil Clark
Managing Editor Amanda Askew
Designer Liz Wiffen